# Contents

# Keeping safe

Electricity can be dangerous.

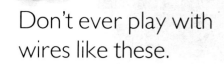

Don't ever play with wires like these.

Never push anything into a socket like this, unless it is a plug.

Never touch plugs or switches if you have wet hands.

Do not have wires where people can trip over them.

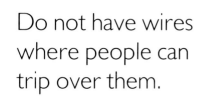

Do not try to mend something which plugs into an electricity socket. If something in your house needs fixing, only a grown-up should try to fix it.

# Llewelyn Peter James Maguire

Llewelyn Peter James Maguire
Touched a live electric wire
Back on his heels it sent him rocking –
His language (like the wire) was shocking!

Cyril Fletcher

Can you find some of the dangers on the next page?

# The mouse who knew better

Mouse knew better!
Do you?
What dangers can you find?

# Magnets

What is keeping the stickers on the fridge?

Do you think you could take them off the fridge door and stick them on the kitchen door instead?

Paul and Shameen were helping to tidy the classroom. The children in their class had dropped so many things on the floor.

Which things do you think they could pick up with a magnet?

I know, let's use a magnet to pick these things up.

# Things which use batteries

Which of these need batteries?

What do you think will happen as the batteries wear out?

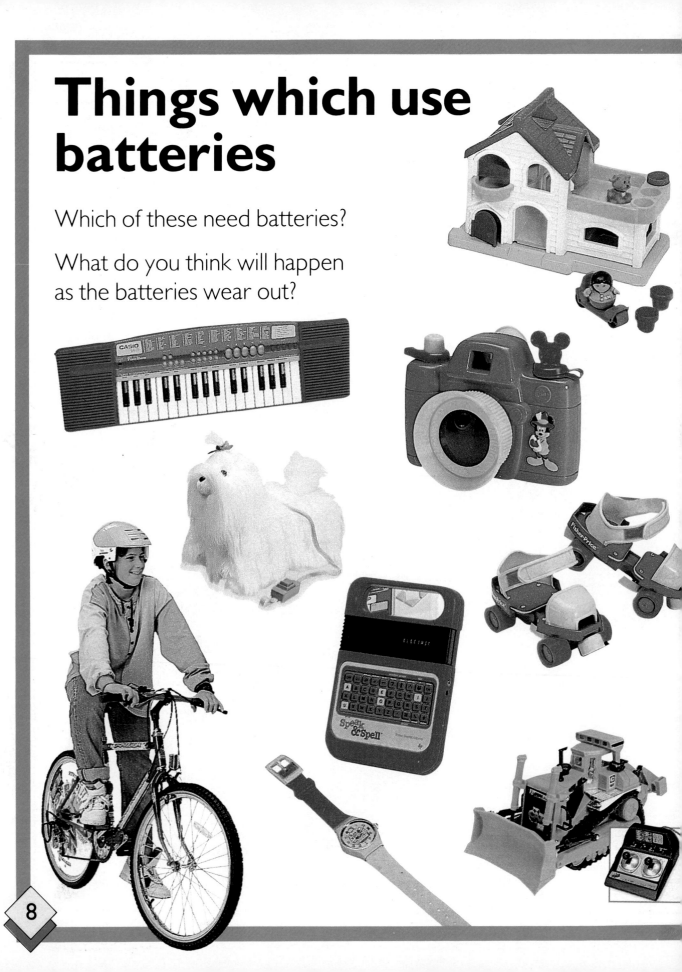

Can you think of some things which you have at home which need batteries to make them work?

# Milk float

A milk float does not sound like other cars and vans. It does not have an exhaust pipe at the back.

The milk float works by electricity. The electricity comes from a very large battery.

**Each night the milk floats are driven back to the garage.**

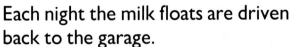

All the batteries have to be re-charged so that they have enough electricity for the next day.

This milk float had to be towed back to the garage because it did not have enough electricity left in its battery.

# Electricity at home

If you leave a light on when you don't need to, it is a waste of energy.

All the electricity we use has to be paid for. You can go to the electricity shop to pay the bill or you can pay it by post.

Turn that light off!

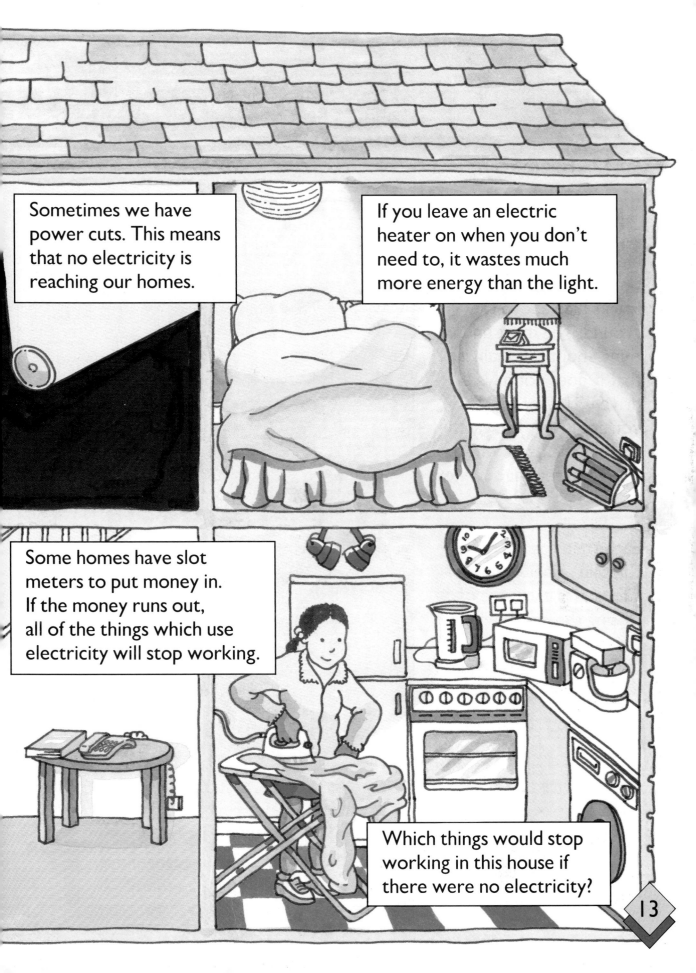

Sometimes we have power cuts. This means that no electricity is reaching our homes.

If you leave an electric heater on when you don't need to, it wastes much more energy than the light.

Some homes have slot meters to put money in. If the money runs out, all of the things which use electricity will stop working.

Which things would stop working in this house if there were no electricity?

13

The Docklands Light Railway works by using electricity. Most of the time the train runs on tracks high above the ground. The most unusual thing about this train is that it does not have a driver. This means that if you are lucky, you can sit right at the front where you get a really good view.

Each train has a 'Train Captain'. The 'Train Captain' is in charge of closing the doors when the passengers have finished getting on and off.

The trains go to and fro along the track, not round and round a circular track.

Railways are dangerous. Don't play on them.

# ight Railway

South Quay

The people in the control room also make sure that it is safe for the train to go. They can make announcements over a loudspeaker if they see anything dangerous.

As there is no driver, how do you think the train stops at the stations?

# Where does electricity come from?

Electricity comes from power stations.

This power station uses coal. It takes a lot of coal to make electricity. The smoke from the coal goes into the air and pollutes it.

power station

This is a nuclear power station. Nuclear power can be dangerous. The people who work at the power station have to make sure that all the machinery is safe and working properly.

The electricity from the power station goes along cables. Some of the cables are underground. Some of them are above the ground on pylons.

The electricity in the cables is very dangerous and can kill anyone who touches a cable. Every year some children die because they try to climb up pylons.

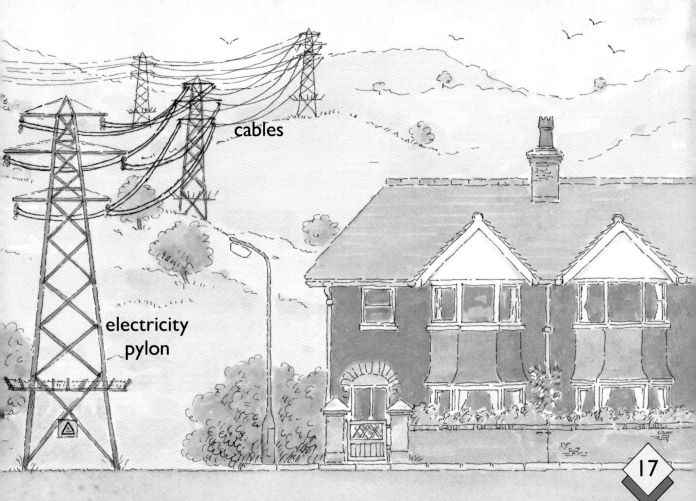

cables

electricity pylon

# Switch it on!

Here are some things which use electricity.
Can you see where the switches are?

How many switches do you have to press
to make them work?

# Electricity in the street

## Which of the things in this street use electricity?

# One hundred years ago

Do you sometimes wonder what life was like a long time ago?

One hundred years ago, you might have had some of these in your home. This was before most homes had electricity.

Can you match the old-fashioned things to the things we have now which use electricity?

# Index

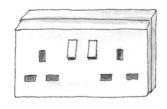
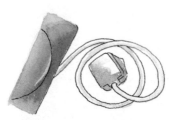